Healing Your Hidden Hurts

Healing Your Hidden Hurts

Tommy,

May God bless ya!

Stephen N. Rummage

Jer. 33:3

Stephen N. Rummage

NORTHEASTERN BAPTIST PRESS

Table of Contents

Acknowledgments   i

Introduction   v

Chapter 1   Facing Your Fears   1

Chapter 2   I Am Not Angry!   17

Chapter 3   Lifting the Veil of Grief   33

Chapter 4   What? Me Worry?   47

Chapter 5   Alone in a Crowd   65

Chapter 6   Crimes and Misdemeanors   79

Chapter 7   What's Your Problem?   93

Acknowledgments

Healing Your Hidden Hurts is a book project I have wanted to complete for many years, and I am very thankful to God for the people who have been instrumental in bringing this book to publication.

Longtime pastor, leader, and Baptist statesman Dr. Bobby Welch encouraged me over a decade ago to preach a series of messages with the title *Healing Your Hidden Hurts*. He reminded me that every congregation is filled with people who are hurting and need a healing word from God. This book is the result of that sermon series, and I am grateful for Brother Bobby's insightful suggestion.

Kim Jackson, program director for the *Moving Forward with Dr. Stephen Rummage* broadcast ministry, once again has accomplished the difficult task of transcribing my preached messages, editing them for clarity, and overseeing the entire process of producing this publication. Without her, this book would never have seen the light of day.

Donna Murrah, my administrative assistant, has provided valuable help in proofreading, making changes to the various drafts, and, extremely significant, keeping me on schedule.

My friend, Perry Kosieniak, designed the layout and formatted the book's contents, diligently poring over every page, and all on a volunteer basis.

Moving Forward listeners have responded appreciatively to these messages when they have been aired on the radio, which was a great motivation for getting *Healing Your Hidden Hurts* into an expanded format in print.

I praise the Lord for the congregation I serve, Quail Springs Baptist Church. My publishing and broadcasting ministries are extensions of my primary calling: to shepherd and preach God's Word in the local church. I feel blessed every day because of this wonderful fellowship of believers who follow Christ faithfully and for the ministers and church staff at Quail Springs.

I am thankful for every preacher, commentator, and author whose work has helped me in proclaiming the messages found in the book. While I have sought to document direct quotations and references, there are countless other resources to which I am indebted as I have prepared.

Finally, I am thankful for my precious wife, Michele. She never stops encouraging me, and her commitment to serve the Lord Jesus with me has made the journey of ministry a joy, even during seasons of testing and difficulty. Our conversations together about life, those we care for, and the struggles people face have helped me to have a greater understanding of the hurts so many of us carry.

To God alone be the glory!

Stephen Rummage

The Pastor's Study
Quail Springs Baptist Church
Oklahoma City, Oklahoma
2022

Introduction

Where Does it Still Hurt?

———————

My parents still talk about it to this day.

When I was a little boy, three or four years old, they would watch as I played in the backyard or ran around on our patio. On occasion, I would stumble and fall, and hit hard on the grass or the pavement with my knees. Mom and Dad say I did the same thing each time. I would get up quickly and check my kneecaps for any damage, looking for signs of blood. If I had on long pants, I would even push up my pantlegs until I could see my knees.

If no blood was showing on my kneecaps, I would return to whatever game I was playing, still happy and unbothered. If, however, the skin was broken and there was even a slight trace of bleeding on my skinned knee, I would begin crying for my mom or dad to come help. In the mind of that little boy, no blood meant the hurt wasn't serious enough to pay attention to. Only the hurt that showed really mattered.

A few years passed and my activities in the backyard became more adventurous. One Sunday afternoon, a friend and I were climbing a tree on the edge of my parents' property. Our game was simple: We'd climb to the highest branch we could reach, and then jump off the limb onto a pile of leaves we had gathered below. In our imaginations, we were jumping for our lives from the second floor of a burning building. In reality, though, we were no more than four feet off the ground.

On one of my jumps from the tree, my foot got caught on a limb, and I wound up plunging toward the ground, headfirst. Instinctively I shot out my left arm to break my fall. When I landed, I felt a sharp pain right below my wrist. I looked down. There was no bleeding anywhere. But something had happened that I could not see. Beneath the skin, hidden, was a broken bone that began to throb and swell. Unlike a skinned knee, no blood was showing. And also, unlike a skinned knee, I wasn't in control of whether I would stop and cry or whether I would get back up and play. The unseen hurt would not go away. I couldn't keep going or stop the pain or turn off the tears. And even ten thousand kisses from my sweet mother's lips would not make it better.

Hidden hurts are often the most serious, most painful, and most lingering problems in our lives. These are very real spiritual scars we try to forget or ignore, damaged emotions we pretend are okay, inner consequences of past sins we try to keep secret or concealed. But, just like a broken bone that causes pain and swelling beneath the skin, or, worse yet, like a hidden, cancerous tumor that grows and metastasizes, hidden hurts can cause deep damage to every part of our lives.

The beauty of our God is that He is able to heal all our hidden hurts, not only the ones that we try to conceal, but, miraculously, even the ones that remain hidden to us. Psalm 103:2–4 says this about God's healing:

> "Bless the Lord, O my soul, And forget not all His benefits:
> Who forgives all your iniquities,
> Who heals all your diseases,
> Who redeems your life from destruction, Who crowns you with lovingkindness and tender mercies."

God forgives sin. God heals pain. God's love redeems our lives from destruction and crowns our heads with His mercy. A word from His lips and a touch from His hand can bring healing to our deep, unseen hurts. Psalm 147:3 bears witness to this same wonderful truth:

> "He heals the brokenhearted And binds up their wounds."

Healing Your Hidden Hurts is a scriptural examination of some of the deepest pains we all feel, hurts such as …

» Fears that cripple and consume us.

> » Anger that damages relationships with people we cherish.
> » Grief that holds us in its grip and robs us of joy.
> » Worry that dominates our thoughts and strangles our faith.
> » Loneliness that makes us feel abandoned and forgotten.
> » Guilt that chains us to the sins of our past.

As we examine God's Word concerning each of these areas of pain, we will discover that God offers us healing, grace, and release.

The messages in each chapter are all "life–tested." As a pastor and a preacher, I have had opportunity to share these messages from the platforms of churches across the country through my radio Bible teaching ministry, *Moving Forward,* as well as individually with people who are struggling with pain. I have found the message of *Healing Your Hidden Hurts* resonates strongly with people, not because I am the most skilled at dealing with these issues, but because these hurts are so intensely felt that people are aching for someone to simply address them.

My prayer is that God will use *Healing Your Hidden Hurts* to encourage you and to help you minister to others who are hurting. Most, though not all, of the chapters are expositions of different portions of the Book of Psalms, the section of Scripture that speaks so powerfully to our pain, our emotions, and our longing for God to meet us at our point of need.

As you read, I would encourage you to do several things:

First, open your own Bible and read the portion of God's Word presented in each chapter. The content and context of the Bible passage itself will speak to you far more powerfully than anything I present in this book. There also may be verses that you will want to mark in your Bible to help remind you of the truths *Healing Your Hidden Hurts* presents.

Second, when you finish reading each chapter, spend some time in prayer asking God: "Father, is there hurt in my life that remains hidden? Give me your grace to uncover that hurt and bring it to you so that You can heal and strengthen me." This book cannot heal your hurts, but it can help direct you to the only One who heals, our God. You will find Him in His Word and through prayer.

Third, as you are praying, ask for the Lord to show you people in your life who may be struggling with these and other hidden hurts. Ask for God to give you wisdom and courage to share His love and mercy with them.

God is so good! He sees what we cannot see. He loves in ways we could never love. He heals perfectly as we bring our hurts to Him. Sometimes that healing comes instantly. More often, I have found that His healing for hidden hurts comes day by day as we trust Him and seek Him with our hearts.

Chapter 1
Facing Your Fears

Psalm 56

"Be merciful to me, O God, for man would swallow me up;
Fighting all day he oppresses me.
My enemies would hound me all day, For there are many
who fight against me, O Most High.
Whenever I am afraid, I will trust in You.
In God (I will praise His word),
In God I have put my trust; I will not fear. What can flesh
do to me?
All day they twist my words;
All their thoughts are against me for evil.
They gather together,
They hide, they mark my steps,
When they lie in wait for my life.
Shall they escape by iniquity?

In anger cast down the peoples, O God!
You number my wanderings; Put my tears into Your bottle;
    Are they not in Your book?
When I cry out to You, Then my enemies will turn back;
This I know, because God is for me.
In God (I will praise His word),
In the Lord (I will praise His word),
In God I have put my trust; I will not be afraid.
What can man do to me?
Vows made to You are binding upon me, O God; I will
    render praises to You, For You have delivered my soul
    from death.
Have You not kept my feet from falling,
That I may walk before God
In the light of the living?"

When I travel for a preaching or other ministry engagement, this would not be an unusual day for me: I wake up around 4:00 a.m. and walk into the bathroom. I'm surprised and a little bothered to see a spider in the corner, looking for his breakfast. So, I use a wad of tissue to grab the spider, and thank the Lord out loud that I didn't miss.

After I've showered and dressed, I kiss Michele goodbye and head through the traffic for the airport, where I wait among hundreds of strangers for my flight. When it's time, I board and settle in with a plane full of other passengers seated shoulder to shoulder. Then, in just a few minutes I'm miles above the earth, trying not to think about the bad weather that's making the plane bump like the atmosphere is full of potholes.

When we finally land, I grab a rental car. Two bridges and a tunnel later, I arrive at my hotel and check in. Door key in hand, I push the button for the elevator. When the elevator door opens, there are five expressionless people already on board, headed to their rooms. I step in, sheepishly make my way to the back of the elevator, and am slowly shuttled to the twelfth floor, where I disembark and head down the hallway to my room to freshen up before my meeting. Then I run over my notes one last time before departing for a conference where I'm one of the scheduled speakers. All the way there, I'm praying that the group of people I'll be speaking to will be gracious if I make a mess out of my words.

Now, a day like that almost always ends up just fine. But the interesting thing is that from the time I wake up that day until that day is done, I will have faced these nine most common phobias listed by Americans:

> Bugs, mice, snakes and bats (that's just one category)
> Heights
> Water
> Public transportation and flying
> Storms
> Tight spaces
> Tunnels or bridges

Crowds
Public speaking

You may be afraid of all of those things; you may not fear any of them. But everyone fears something.

Truth is, fear can be your friend. Fear is a protective response that God has designed to assist us when we are endangered. Our bodies release adrenaline when we face danger to help us move more quickly and with greater strength in perilous situations.

But fear can also be one of your greatest enemies. Fear has the ability to paralyze you, making you incapable of acting. Fear can dominate your life, consume your thoughts, and distract your attention. Fear can even kill you.

Dr. Robert Kloner at the Good Samaritan Hospital in Los Angeles studied the rates of heart attacks on the day of the 1994 earthquakes in that city. He found that there were five times the number of heart attacks reported than there were on the same day in other years. Dr. Kloner said that about a hundred Californians died that day because of fear. Fear released chemicals into their bodies, triggering such a severe contraction of the heart that it never relaxed.[1]

Most people don't literally die from fear, but many are crippled by it. God wants to strengthen you to walk in victory over your fears, whatever they are. As we look at Psalm 56, we can see three principles from God's Word that will

---

1   https://www.nytimes.com/1996/02/15/us/jump–in–fatal-heart– attacks–is–tied–to–quake.html, Warren E Leary, February 15, 1996

help you step out in faith to do what God has called you to do, even when you face great fear.

First, God wants you to come to grips with the *reality of fear* in your life. Next, God calls you to a *reaction of faith* when your fears are raging. Finally, God reminds you of the *requirement of following* Him through your fears. Let's consider each of those principles as we examine this portion of God's Word.

THE REALITY OF FEAR

"Fighting all day he oppresses me.
My enemies would hound me all day,
For there are many who fight against me, O Most High."
                                             Psalm 56:1–2

Every person is, at one time or another, confronted by things that make us afraid. David was. In the Bible we see that David cried out many times to God for grace and mercy because of fear. He asked for God to listen to him and to see him. And he asked God to reach down to him and do something in his life.

David asked this question: What can flesh do to me? What can man do to me?

Of course, men (and women, for that matter) can do a lot of things to make us afraid. Some of our biggest fears are not airplanes, earthquakes, spiders, or bugs, but the hurts caused by other people.

David found himself being pursued by enemies who were trying to hurt him. The Scripture says David's enemies wanted to *swallow him up*. That means they wouldn't give up until they got him. His opponents were relentless. They intended to *oppress him* – to press him down until he was crushed. The language David uses paints a picture of a pack of merciless hyenas after a gazelle. The predators will not give up the hunt, and their intent is nothing short of destruction.

David had first–hand experience with this kind of assault. The ancient superscription to this Psalm, as ancient as the Psalm itself, tells us that David wrote these words when he had been captured by the Philistines in Gath, the hometown of Goliath, the giant whom David had conquered and killed years before. Goliath was no longer a problem, but the king of Israel, Saul, was. Saul and his men were in hot pursuit of David, but not because David had done anything wrong. To the contrary, he had done everything right and had become increasingly popular in the eyes of the people of Israel. King Saul became a mad man, driven to a jealousy–fueled hatred of David.

As he fled from Saul, David ran to a priest named Ahimelech and begged for food and protection. Ahimelech was of little help to David, but he gave him all that he had: the sword of Goliath and the bread devoted to the Lord's service in the tabernacle.

David probably didn't look like much of a threat as he dragged Goliath's huge sword through the streets of Gath. But he was under constant threat from his enemies. So, he devised a plan: he would feign insanity. David thought, "If I act crazy, they'll leave me alone."

But David's plan actually brought him more trouble. The king of Gath said something like this: "Look, I've got enough crazy people to deal with already. Somebody get rid of this guy!" Now David was running from multiple pursuers: the men of Gath, as well as Saul and his men.

There was nothing easy about David's situation. He describes what he was experiencing in Psalm 56:5–6:

> "All day they twist my words;
> All their thoughts are against me for evil.
> They gather together,
> They hide, they mark my steps,
> When they lie in wait for my life."

David was alone, under attack, vulnerable, panicked, and afraid. His situation was dire and the threats against him were very real.

David was probably a wreck: heart pounding; dry mouth; tense muscles; nerves on edge; a queasy stomach; profuse sweat. Fear produces a real, visceral response. Fear can make you physically sick and exhaust you.

Now, here's what may surprise you: As far as we can tell, David was right in the center of God's will. Yes, David was under attack. He was alone and he was scared – and right where he was supposed to be.

Fear is a fact of life, and it pops up when you least expect it. We try many strategies to deal with fear: We may try to ignore it, or adopt an I–don't–care attitude. Sometimes we try to paint a brave face on our fear, or maintain a false show of confidence.

But God always knows – and you know – when you are afraid.

A mother tucked her little boy into bed one windy, stormy night. Lightning flashed and thunder boomed just outside the window. He was very scared.

He said to his mother, "Mommy, can you please stay in my room and sleep with me tonight?" She said, "No honey, I have to go and sleep in Daddy's room tonight." There was a long pause. The boy lowered his eyes, crossed his arms, and said, "That big chicken."

Sometimes, you're going to be afraid, even when you're in exactly the right place, at the right time, doing the right thing. So, the question is not *"Will I be afraid?"* The question is *"What will I do when I am afraid?"*

Not long ago, I faced a situation where I was extremely fearful. I was unsure about how people would treat me and uncertain about my future. In those moments and days, a piece of simple advice that a wise, older Christian man gave me proved powerful and comforting in my life. My friend told me: "Put this in the Lord's hands. Let Him take care of it." That simple word of encouragement helped me to move from the reality of my fear into a reaction of faith.

THE REACTION OF FAITH

Psalm 56:3–4 records this faith response of David:

> "Whenever I am afraid, I will trust in You.
> In God (I will praise His word),
> In God I have put my trust;
> I will not fear."

In spite of David's fear, he made a conscious decision to trust God. Instead of letting fear rule his life, David chose to hold tightly to God and not let go. Why could he do that? Verse 4 tells us David trusted God's character and God's Word:

> "In God (I will praise His Word), in God I have put
> my trust."

In effect, David was saying, "I know God's Word is true. He's spoken to me in His Word and told me not to be afraid, so that's what I'm going to do: I'm going to not be afraid." The decision was just as simple as that.

Another reason David refused to fear is found in Psalm 56:7. About his enemies David says,

> "Shall they escape by iniquity?
> In anger cast down the peoples, O God!"

David had total confidence that God would take care of the people who were trying to hurt him. He knew that God's righteous anger would deal with those who were trying to harm him, and that God had the supernatural ability to remove David's enemies from before him.

David also knew that God was watching his every step. In Psalm 56:8, David creates this striking word picture of God's care:

> "You number my wanderings; Put my tears into Your
>   bottle.
> Are they not in Your book?"

God even saved every tear that David shed, like entries in a memory book.

Sometimes our fears become so great and consuming that we start to feel that the best way to deal with them is simply to forget. We push the bad times and the tears we shed into the far recesses of our memories and promise ourselves never even to think about them again. God's love for us is so great, though, that He never forgets. He numbers our days of fearful wandering, and even keeps every tear we shed in His bottle of remembrance.

If you've wept because of your fears, God has saved your tears in a bottle with your name on it. Your tears are precious to Him. He cares that tenderly for you.

David knew that because of God's tender love for Him, God was in His corner! In Psalm 56:9, he writes,

"When I cry out to You,
Then my enemies will turn back.
This I know, because God is for me."

David was certain that God heard his prayers. He was sure that God would rout even the fiercest of his enemies. Above all, David knew that God was for him.

Never forget that God is for you! You may feel that everyone is against you, even those closest to you. But God is for you. And because of that, you can say with David,

"In God (I will praise His word), in the Lord (I will praise His word),
In God I have put my trust; I will not be afraid."

PSALM 56:10–11

The acronym "FEAR" has been used by many people to stand for "False Evidence Appearing Real." But sometimes the evidence isn't false; it's very real!

Here's what I think "FEAR" stands for:

Forgetting Everything's All Right!

That is so easy for us to do when we become afraid. We forget who God is. We forget where God is. We forget what God has promised. In short, we forget that – because we belong to God – everything really is all right.

Several years ago, our family went to Carowinds amusement park in North Carolina. Michele's parents and sister joined us, and we had a great day together. By late afternoon, I think I had ridden every ride in that park, including all the roller coasters, except one.

A Star Trek–themed coaster called "The Borg Assimilator" was the only roller coaster I had not ridden. And I just didn't think God was calling me at that moment to get "assimilated," or to "boldly go where no man has gone before," even though I saw lots of men, women, and eight-year-old kids waiting in line for the ride!

I had watched hundreds of people get onboard the Assimilator. All the riders were loaded onto the roller coaster lying on their backs, with their heads pointed toward the front of the ride. When the ride started it took them slowly up the first hill backward: *katunk, katunk, katunk.*

Then at the top of that hill, the Assimilator flipped the riders over like a pancake, and for the rest of the ride they were suspended by a harness, and flying through every twist and turn of that roller coaster, face down. A net under the Assimilator caught things that fell: glasses, hats, wallets. I thought to myself, "I don't want to end up in that net. I'm not riding the Borg Assimilator."

That was my final decision, until Michele said, "Stephen, ride that with my daddy."

Michele's dad, Aubrey Henderson, was about seventy-two years old at the time. I dearly love my father-in-law, and I love my wife even more. So, I got in line with him, right behind a little girl about nine years old. Aubrey was so excited, and that little girl was also excited. Everyone in the line was excited but me. I spent forty–five anxiety–laced minutes in that line trying to remember that everything would be all right.

When our turn to ride finally came, Aubrey and I were buckled into our harnesses, side by side. As we were ascending the first hill, he yelled at me: "Stephen, you're not looking! Look around! You can see all kinds of things!" I wasn't looking. My eyes were squeezed shut in fear. I said, "Aren't you scared?" He said, "I'm not scared of one ride in this park!"

I was thinking about my harness breaking, and falling into that net, and being out of control. I had forgotten that everything was all right. In the end, I was assimilated that day and came out no worse for the wear. The harness held, and I survived.

Everything was all right.

In a much deeper way, when life turns everything upside down, we may fear for our future and well being. However, when we face our fears, whether they are great or small, we are reminded, once again, that Jesus makes everything all right.

At the cross of Calvary, Jesus faced our biggest fears and defeated them all. As a result, everything is all right. Jesus defeated His earthly enemies, so everything's all right! He defeated Satan; everything's all right! He defeated death, so everything's all right! He defeated sin, so everything's all right! He defeated hell, so everything's all right!

When you wonder how things are going to turn out in your situation, you can cry out to God in faith: "Lord, in the middle of this fear, I'm going to cling to You. I trust You. I'm not letting go of You, and I know You won't let go of me. So, everything is all right."

THE REQUIREMENT OF FOLLOWING

At the end of this Psalm, David expressed his intention to keep following the Lord, even after his fears had been defeated. He wrote in Psalm 56:12– 13:

> "Vows made to You are binding upon me, O God; I
>   will render praises to You, For You have delivered
>   my soul from death.
> Have You not kept my feet from falling,
> That I may walk before God
> In the light of the living?"

David made promises, or vows, to God when he was fearful. Sometimes we call those kinds of promises "foxhole prayers." They usually go something like this: *God, if you'll* _____ *for me, then I'll* _____ *for you.* You can fill in the blanks.

Now that the danger had passed, David determined to keep his vows to God. He declared they were binding upon him. No matter what happened in the future, David promised to live his life praising God, and keeping the promises he made when he was afraid.

Have you made vows to God when you were afraid? When you were in the hospital and didn't think you were going to come out? Or when you wept over the bed of a loved one you feared losing? What have you promised God when you faced a financial crisis that you feared you could not overcome? Or when you were threatened on your job?

Too often after rescue has come and danger has passed, we leave our promises by the wayside. The old saying is sadly true: "Danger gone; God forgotten."

David didn't forget God after the danger had passed. He kept his vows made during danger. He spent his life praising God and following Him. Was he perfect? No, not by a long stretch! But he was faithful to his promise to follow God, to praise Him, and to walk with the Lord for the rest of his life.

Can the same be said of you?

A man spent several days and nights on the Texas prairie with a shepherd who was managing a flock of about two thousand sheep. He watched the shepherd work hard to care for the sheep under the hot sun. As darkness descended, the entire flock gathered around the shepherd and lay down to rest. The shepherd had built a fire for warmth and light in the center of where his flock lay. Everyone was at rest after a long day.

Then the sheep dogs became restless. They patrolled among the sheep and began to growl as the unmistakable wails of coyotes pierced the peace of the prairie. The unseen enemy posed a real threat to the flock.

The shepherd sprang into action. He tossed more wood onto the fire, which blazed brighter and higher. As the light from the fire grew, the man looked into the night, where he saw thousands of tiny lights encircling their camp. He realized that what he was seeing was the firelight being reflected in the eyes of the two thousand sheep, who were looking, not into the darkness, but toward their shepherd.

The secret to successfully facing your fears is realizing that Jesus Christ has already faced them all for you. Your Good Shepherd will protect you. So, when doubts arise and fears dismay, look to Jesus and to His cross. He has promised to deliver you from whatever makes you afraid.

Chapter 2
I Am Not Angry!

"Rest in the Lord, and wait patiently for Him;
Do not fret because of him who prospers in his way, Because
of the man who brings wicked schemes to pass.
Cease from anger, and forsake wrath; Do not fret – it only
causes harm.
For evildoers shall be cut off;
But those who wait on the Lord,
They shall inherit the earth."

PSALM 37:7–9

Has this happened to you? You're in a room, and in walks another person – maybe your spouse, or child, or even a friend. And as soon as you look at the person's face, you know something's wrong. Their lips are pursed;

you can hear forced exhalations; the person seems tense from head to toe. Something's not right. So you ask, *"What's wrong?"* And the response is this: *"Nothing."*

Though you know you ought to leave the situation alone, you continue to ask questions. *"Are you sure everything's okay?"* *"Are you angry about something?"* And then, in clipped tones, the person says, *"I'm NOT angry."* *"Everything's okay"* comes the answer. Instead, the person may give you a list of other emotions, all very closely related to anger.

"I'm frustrated."
"I'm irritated."
"I'm annoyed."
"I'm flustered."
"I'm upset."
"I'm hurt."
"I'm disappointed."

But still, the person insists with defiant emphasis: "I am <u>not</u> angry."

Especially in Christian circles, we are often hesitant to admit that we are struggling with anger. Perhaps it's because we mistakenly think that all anger is sin, or that Christ–like love and kindness prohibits us from ever feeling or expressing anger. And so, we call our anger something else, such as hurt or disappointment or frustration, and we never deal with the reality of our anger.

The Bible is very upfront about the presence of anger within our relationships, and even our anger toward God.

As I began writing this chapter, football season was just around the corner. Here's what I've observed about football: People wear the expensive jerseys, drive long distances, and pay top prices just to watch their team and be angry. At the players. At the refs. At the coaches. At the concession prices. At the lines at the restroom.

It's not just at football games. Anger is on display in all kinds of places: on the highway; in the checkout line at the grocery store; at our dinner tables; on social media; in the workplace; and even at church. Often, the places where we display our anger are not the cause of our anger. Instead, these circumstances are only our excuse to expose the embedded anger that has grown a much deeper and destructive root in our lives.

Psalm 37:7–9 provides a penetrating and insightful portrayal of how anger operates in the human heart, and what we can do to deal with our anger in a way that pleases God.

THE REASONS FOR ANGER

David gives sage advice in Psalm 37:7:

"Do not fret because of him who prospers in his way,
Because of the man who brings wicked schemes to
    pass."

It's very important to understand that not all anger is wrong. God has wired us to feel outrage and anger in some circumstances.

Anger is justified when we witness injustice, whether it happens to someone else, or to us.

That's what David is writing about in Psalm 37. He sees wicked people hurting other people. They spend their lives creating and carrying out wicked schemes. And instead of the wicked person getting his just desserts, he's doing better than most. In fact, the Bible says he prospers.

Doesn't it get under your skin and doesn't it make you really *angry* when you see someone getting ahead by treating others unjustly? How do you respond to the kid who always cheats on his tests and yet makes straight A's? The co–worker who lies her way into promotions? The businessman who steals from the company but never gets caught? Anger is a God–given response to that type of injustice. God has created us to be outraged when we see the wicked prospering.

In fact, God is angry at those things, too. Psalm 7:11 says,

> "God is a just judge, and God is angry with the wicked every day."

God is offended when He sees the wicked prosper. Because we are created in His image, we also experience outrage at corruption.

Later in this Psalm, David expressed anger because the wicked in Israel oppressed the poor. Psalm 37:12 and 14 describe what was happening:

"The wicked plots against the just,
And gnashes at him with his teeth."
"The wicked have drawn the sword And have bent
    their bow,
To cast down the poor and needy,
To slay those who are of upright conduct."

Injustice in the world is nothing new. From biblical times, the wicked have taken advantage of the poor, the helpless, the needy, and the righteous. The God–given reaction to that kind of mistreatment is anger.

Even small examples of wrongdoing can awaken our anger. One year, Michele and I took our son, Joshua, to Disney World for his birthday. We were there all day long. It was hot, and it was crowded, but we were happy, because, after all, Disney is the happiest place on earth. Except at closing time.

At the end of the day, we made our way to the tram station and got in line with thousands of our best friends to wait our turn to board. Of course, no one is tired or irritable at the end of the day, because it's Disney! Can you detect my sarcasm? Everyone was tired, and most of us were a little irritable, or at least on edge.

We had waited almost a half hour in line, when a guy came out of nowhere and pushed his way onto the tram, knocking out of the way people ahead of us who had waited a long time. He pushed one guy off the tram, and then another, whose family was already on the tram. The tension and the anger started to boil over. Those two guys got chest to chest and about came to blows right there in the Magic Kingdom.

The other passengers stood up for the guy whose family was on the tram and shamed the encroacher into giving up his seat and letting the guy back on. Then he crammed himself back into the seat, and away they went.

I don't know what happened on the other end of their journey. I'm glad I wasn't there to find out. But everyone was pretty angry with this guy. Why? Because he had done a wrong and still got what he wanted.

Maybe you grew up in a home where your dad was a tyrant and abused your mom. Maybe he abused you. No one had to tell you that it wasn't right; you knew. That mistreatment planted a seed of anger inside of you as a child. You probably didn't even realize it at the time. But it grew. Perhaps your anger has hardened into bitterness and even hatred.

So now, when you're taken advantage of, or you see other people getting ahead unfairly, you explode.

Maybe someone you love is sick, and it makes you angry. Maybe you're angry at God, or at the doctors. And you say, "It's not fair! This shouldn't happen!"

Anger is a normal response that we feel when we perceive that the world is not right. When we see injustice, evil, and mistreatment go unpunished or even rewarded, it awakens again. In itself, anger is not sinful.

However, we must learn to deal with our anger God's way, because it can become very harmful when our anger leads us into sin.

THE RISK OF OUR ANGER

In Psalm 37:8, David gives this command,

> "Cease from anger, and forsake wrath; Do not fret – it
> only causes harm."

In this verse, three distinct words are used to describe our outrage.

The first is the word *anger*. In the Hebrew language, the word translated *anger* actually means *nose*. Literally, the verse says, "Cease from nose."

What does this strange figure of speech mean? Well, when a person is angry, the nose often burns or tingles. Remember the angry person who walked into the room, and the forced exhalations you heard? That's what the Bible is talking about here. So, the Bible literally encourages us to not let our nose burn. It's a warning against the physical risks of uncontrolled anger.

There are obvious physiological manifestations of anger: beads of sweat on the forehead; clinched fists; grinding teeth; tight jaw. Have you ever felt better physically because of your anger? No! Uncontrolled, sustained anger can become harmful to our bodies.

The second word used in this text for anger is *wrath*. The Bible commands us to forsake wrath. The Hebrew word for *wrath* is easier to understand; it means venom or poison. Wrath is like poison coursing through the veins. Raging anger affects us not only on the outside, but on the inside of our bodies. Heart pounding; stomach churning; blood pressure rising. Those things are not good for you.

Then the text says that we are not to *fret*. The word *fret* means to burn. The term is similar in meaning to anger – but now more than the nose is burning! Anger can become a consuming fire that inflames our thoughts and emotions and scorches our most treasured relationships.

What are we to do with anger, wrath, and fretting? We are to cease! Consider the words of Psalm 37:8 again:

"Cease from anger …"

The word *cease* here means to go limp. The verse literally says: "*Let your nose hang limp.*" As strange as that imagery sounds, it paints a vivid picture of ceasing from anger. We might say it this way: Let the air out of the tires of your anger. Take the boiling pot of anger off the burner. Stop letting your anger be in control.

The next instruction regarding anger is to forsake our wrath. To *forsake* means to let something go. Turn it loose. Drop it.

Some people carry around a cargo of anger in their hearts and minds. It's hurting you, and it will hurt your family. It cannot be stated too strongly: You need to forsake your wrath. Let it go. Quit fretting. It only causes harm, and lots of it.

❦

Several years ago, I found in the back of my closet an old boom–box I used in the eighties. Boom–boxes with big speakers were really cool in the eighties, and I always enjoyed using mine. So, I decided that I would take it to my office and use it again.

I plugged that boom–box into an outlet and turned it on. Nothing happened. The radio didn't work. Neither would the cassette player work. So, I investigated, and when I pried open the battery compartment, I found batteries that I had left in there years ago. The acid from the batteries had seeped out and corroded the inner workings of the radio. It was destroyed.

That's such a good picture of what happens inside of us when we leave our anger unchecked. It not only eats away at you; it will seep out onto other people and hurt them.

The Bible brings wisdom to the issue of anger that should be heeded. Not only should we be on guard against our own uncontrolled anger. We also need to be aware of risks of entering close relationships with other people who are carrying a load of anger. Proverbs 22:24–25 says,

> "Make no friendship with an angry man, and with a
>   furious man do not go,
> Lest you learn his ways and set a snare for your soul."

This wisdom is for all of your relationships. Don't marry someone who angrily lashes out at you or others. Don't make a bitter person your business partner. Don't go on vacation with angry people. Don't walk arm in arm with a furious man or woman, because you will learn their ways. It will rub off on you and ensnare your soul.

There are warnings in almost every book of the Bible about anger. Jesus and Paul both talked about the danger of anger. One of the most helpful portions of Scripture about the risks of anger is found in James 1:19–20:

> "So then, my beloved brethren, let every man be swift
>   to hear, slow to speak, slow to wrath; for the wrath
>   of man does not produce the righteousness of
>   God."

The principle here is simple: Our wrath, our uncontrolled anger, never pleases God or produces what God desires in our lives. That truth from God's Word wipes away all of the flimsy excuses we try to offer for unrestrained anger. We may say, *"I get my temper naturally." "Everyone in my family gets mad like I do." "I'm like my dad." "I'm like my grandmother."* A short temper does not produce the righteousness of God, no matter where it came from.

Or we may say, *"I just have a short fuse. I explode, then I'm over it."* A nuclear bomb does the same thing: It explodes and then it's done, but it does enormous harm. A short fuse does not produce the righteousness of God.

The words we release in anger may relieve the pressure we're feeling, but people we spew them on can be destroyed by them – a spouse, our kids, our family or even a church.

If you refuse to let go of anger, then you are a walking bomb, waiting to explode and cause destruction all around. Anger is risky business.

THE RELEASE OF OUR ANGER

Psalm 37:7 says,

"Rest in the Lord, and wait patiently for Him."

According to this verse, there are two remedies for our anger: rest and patience.

God created us with all kinds of muscles in our bodies. But He has not created one muscle strong enough to bear the burden of our own anger. In order to be released from our anger, God calls us to rest in Him and to wait for Him to take care of the situation that is causing us hurt and anger.

But we might protest: What about the wrongdoing or injustice that made us so angry to begin with? What about the wicked person who keeps getting away with everything? As Psalm 37 continues, we see that it is not our job to punish evildoers; that's God's job. God is just, holy, and righteous. He will eventually bring perfect, sinless justice to those who wrong you and prosper in spite of it. Psalm 37:9–11 says,

> "For evildoers shall be cut off; But those who wait on
>   the Lord, They shall inherit the earth.
> For yet a little while and the wicked shall be no more;
>   Indeed, you will look carefully for his place, But it
>   shall be no more.
> But the meek shall inherit the earth,
> And shall delight themselves in the abundance of
>   peace."

God *will* deal justly with evildoers who do not repent. The Bible says that He will *cut them off*. Those words can mean that God will totally destroy them. It also means that they will be stopped. God will stop the wicked, in His time, in His way. And, unless they repent and turn to Jesus Christ, evildoers will be totally destroyed. Not a trace of them will be left.

But the meek, those who rest in the Lord and wait for His justice, *will inherit the earth*. That means that the person who trusts God will enjoy God's blessings. When we rest and patiently wait on the Lord to right wrongs, He will. That's why Romans 12:19 tells us,

> "Beloved, do not avenge yourselves, but rather give place to wrath; for it is written, 'Vengeance is Mine, I will repay,' says the Lord."

When we rest in the Lord and place our anger in His loving hands, God works powerfully in our lives to enable us to show His goodness and grace to those who made us angry. Romans 12:21 says,

> "Do not be overcome by evil, but overcome evil with good."

Jesus talked about this very thing in Matthew 5:44–45:

> "But I say to you, love your enemies, bless those who curse you, do good to those who hate you, and pray for those who spitefully use you and persecute you, that you may be sons of your Father in heaven; for He makes His sun rise on the evil and on the good, and sends rain on the just and on the unjust."

As you consider those commands of Jesus, remember: Jesus hasn't asked us to do something He has never done Himself. Jesus loved His enemies – the same people who cursed Him, hated Him, and spitefully persecuted Him. So, He is able to come to your aid and give you all the help you need to do the same to people who hurt you.

When you forgive and love your enemies, the result is that you look like what you are: a child of our Father in heaven.

One way to overcome our anger toward others is to remind ourselves of the anger we deserve from God because of our own sin. When the Bible says in Psalm 7:11,

"God is angry with the wicked every day,"

that includes us in our wickedness.

Think of all the things you've done to offend God, to hurt God, and to break His heart. If God would love you so much that He would forgive you of your many sins, who are you to say: *I will never forgive him. I can never forgive her. I'm not letting this go! I'll carry it to my grave!*

If you've been saved by the blood of Jesus Christ, then you have no right to nurse your anger. Release it. God will take care of it. You can pray for that person and for the circumstance that made you angry, and you will be flooded with relief.

Preacher and author Anthony Campolo tells of a time he was preaching at a church in Oregon. In the morning service, he prayed for a man who was sick and had come to the altar. Later that week, he received a call from the man's wife. She told him that her husband had cancer, and that he had died. Pastor Campolo was heartbroken. He told the woman, "I'm so sorry; I feel so bad."

She said, "Don't feel bad. When my husband came to church Sunday, he was so angry with God. He hated God because of his cancer. He wanted so badly to be with me and our kids and our grandchildren. He was bitter and he cursed God because it just felt so unfair."

She continued, "But when you prayed for him, God moved in his heart and replaced his anger with His joy and peace. These last three days have been the happiest of our marriage We sang together, and read Scripture together. We had time to enjoy our family. My husband didn't get cured, but he did get healed."

You can't undo things that have been done to you. The past is unchangeable, including mistreatment, abuse, disappointment, hurt, and injustice.

But, praise God, your past doesn't have to be your present, and you don't have to carry it into your future! God can totally transform the way you deal with your anger at your past. If you will offload your burden onto Him by faith, He will give you relief and release from your anger.

God may not choose to heal you of your sickness. He may not deliver you from an unjust circumstance. But He will meet you right where you are and release you from the hidden hurt and the anger as you simply say, *Lord, I'm resting in You.* You don't have to carry your anger for one more minute. Rest in Him. Trust in Him.

He will take care of it.

Chapter 3
Lifting the Veil of Grief

"You have turned for me my mourning into dancing; You have put off my sackcloth and clothed me with gladness,

To the end that my glory may sing praise to You and not be silent. O Lord my God, I will give thanks to You forever."

PSALM 30:11–12

I was just twenty–three years old when I started pastoring. To this day, I am amazed that anyone in my first church could pay attention to anything I had to say from the pulpit or follow me as their shepherd. Yet, graciously and patiently, they did recognize the call of God on my life to serve them. Still, my inexperience was impossible to miss. I knew somewhat how to preach a sermon and how to smile and shake hands after the service.

But on my very first day as a pastor, I was called into the unfamiliar territory of grief. I said the very best things I knew to say to Jerry Mitchell's widow and mother. I read the Scripture to them, and I prayed for them. But I was a rookie when it came to dealing with grief and loss.

Fast forward almost twenty years. Michele and I had answered God's call to move to Brandon, Florida, for me to pastor Bell Shoals Baptist Church. On my first Sunday in that pulpit, I faced a grieving congregation whose precious pastor, Forrest Pollock, along with his thirteen-year-old son, Preston, had been killed in a tragic plane crash just months before. Unbelievably, just weeks after the deaths of Forrest and Preston, their beloved worship pastor, Simeon Nix, had died suddenly and unexpectedly. Not only were the families of these men swimming in grief; every member of the congregation shared in the experience of pain and loss.

It doesn't take very long in ministry, or in life itself, to learn firsthand about death, bereavement, profound sorrow, and grief.

I've now preached hundreds of funerals, including the funerals of my two grandmothers and Michele's beloved mother. Michele and I have grieved the loss of a child through miscarriage. I lost my dear friend Mark to cancer, and stood to comfort his wife and young son after he had slipped away to heaven. And Mark is only one friend of many that I have grieved over the years.

Grief is easily defined as pain caused by loss. But there are so many dimensions of grief. It is universal. It is individual. It is both broad and personal. It is shared and it is private. It knocks you down. And just when you think that the heavy waves of grief have subsided, you're blindsided by another that threatens to drag you back into the depths.

Many times, we prefer our grief to stay hidden, like a face behind a veil. When asked how we are, we answer that we're doing fine. We paint smiles over our broken hearts. But we are not doing fine. Grief is relentless and uncomfortable. It makes us feel out of sorts. Grief is sometimes unbearably hard.

But God can transform our lives through grief. Grief can become a tool in God's hand to fashion us increasingly into what He desires for us to become. And, while grief is inescapable, necessary, and even beneficial in seasons of our lives, God wants to restore grieving people to lives of joy and gladness.

Psalm 30 contains an examination of the emotions and experiences of grief, as well as a guide for how to bring our grief to God.

THE EMOTIONS OF GRIEF

David wrote in Psalm 30, verses 3, 7, and 10,

> "O Lord, You brought my soul up from the grave; You have kept me alive, that I should not go down to the pit."

"You hid your face, and I was troubled." "Hear, O
Lord, and have mercy on me; Lord, be my helper!"

Grief can be a sinking feeling. David likens the feeling of grief to plummeting all the way to the bottom of a deep pit, into the realm of the dead.

David said, "You hid Your face, and I was troubled." David wasn't just little bit bothered, not just a tad concerned. The word translated *troubled* indicates that he was terrified deep within his soul.

David felt helpless and vulnerable. His emotions were raw. He felt emotionally exposed. David pleaded for God to be his helper – to encircle and surround him with His presence and to protect him.

Sinking. Terrified. Helpless. Hidden. Vulnerable. Raw. Exposed. Those are the emotions of grief.

There is so much more to grief than the feelings of sadness and sorrow. Grief is complicated. It can produce feelings of anger and bitterness, frustration, impatience, relief, guilt, love, and resentment. Grief is a tornado that swirls with every emotion you can imagine, all at the same time.

Remember when you were a kid and you'd pull a tooth? Before the permanent tooth grew in, there was a big hole inside your mouth. I remember that I stuck my tongue in that hole all the time. I just couldn't ignore it; it felt so big. I was aware of it all the time. Why? Because something was missing, and I was trying to fill it.

Grief is like that. It's a hole left by something or someone important who is missing. At the dinner table. In the car. On the other side of the bed. On the other end of the telephone. Beside you at church.

Who have you lost? Your companion? Your bread-winner? Your housekeeper? Your bookkeeper? Your orga-nizer? The fountain of wisdom you turned to? Your cook? Your mechanic? Your friend? Your lover? Your pride and joy? Your entertainer? The person who understood your private jokes? The person so unique that there is no one else like him or her? The shoulder you cried on? Your comfort-er? The one who understood you best?

Words offered by well–meaning friends can sometimes feel hurtful. "Well, that person really isn't lost; you know where he is." But he's lost to you: You can't see him, or touch him, or hear him. All that other person was to you is gone. Those realities of loss, of someone missing, form the fabric of grief.

When Jesus came to earth, He entered the entire hu-man experience. That included grief. The Bible calls Jesus *a man of sorrows and acquainted with grief.* He wasn't just aware of our grief; Jesus personally knew the experience of grief. You learned that in Sunday school when you memorized the shortest verse in the Bible:

"Jesus wept."

JOHN 11:35

Jesus shed tears over the death of His friend Lazarus. Your closest comforter knows your pain because He has ex-perienced it. The best comforter is the one who has walked the road before you.

A woman's disabled daughter had died. The daughter and mother had lived together all of their lives. They were the best of friends and close companions.

The mother didn't know what to do. The emptiness in her home was palpable, and she was miserable and sad.

She went to visit her pastor. And he said to her, "When you go home and put the key in the front door lock, I want you to say this out loud: "*Jesus is here.*" When you look at her empty chair at the table, say, "*Jesus is here.*" And at the end of the day, I want you to sit and tell Jesus everything about your day. If someone was unkind to you, tell Jesus. If somebody irritated you, tell Jesus about it. Talk to Jesus just like you would have talked to your daughter, and say out loud, "*I know Jesus is here.*""

A few months had passed when the pastor saw this woman again. He saw new joy on her face. She said, "It was so simple, but I did what you said. Every time I come home, I say, "*I know Jesus is here.*" And I talk to Jesus. I know Him so much better now than I knew Him before."

Jesus is ready to meet you at the point of your grief, because He's been there. He will walk with you through every emotion you experience when grief leaves a hole in your life.

THE ENDURING PROCESS OF GRIEF

In Psalm 30:5, David wrote these familiar words,

> "Weeping may endure for a night, But joy comes in
> the morning."

If you have even spent one entire night in tears, you know that can seem like an eternity. Grief settles in and stays for a long while. There are no shortcuts in processing grief.

Michele and I have a friend we grew up with who visited us many times after we were married. We'd eat dinner together, and then go to the den to visit. And she'd stay. And stay. And stay. So, by 10:00 p.m., Michele and I would do things to hint to her that it was time for her to go. I'd say, "I've got to get up really early in the morning." And she'd say, "Me, too!" And she'd stay. Or, I'd look at my watch, yawn, and say, "It's later than I thought it was." She didn't get it. We'd sit on the edges of our seats, hoping she'd do the same thing. But she settled more deeply into her chair. Our friend endured through the night, until she decided it was time for her to go.

Grief is exactly like that. Grief pays no attention to your calendar or your wristwatch. Grief hasn't read the books that talk about the steps of healing and what it should look like. Grief doesn't travel a straight line. Grief moves in an ever–repeating spiral. You may work through issues of grief and pain and think, "*Well I'm done with that.*" only to have the same pains and sense of loss or anger pop up again

… and again … and again. Grief endures. But joy comes in the morning!

If grief is like the guest who stays longer than you want, then joy is like the guest you're anxiously anticipating to arrive. Joy will come! You can look forward to that.

Every person's grief timeline is different. You are not on someone else's grief trajectory, and they are not on yours. Your grief is your own; it is personal to you. If your friends are uncomfortable with your grief, wondering why you just don't get over it, realize this: Your grief is normal for you. And when you have endured, joy will come.

Psalm 6 is a transparently honest prayer that David offered to God in his grief. In Psalm 6:2 and 6:6, he prays,

"Have mercy on me, O Lord, for I am weak;
O Lord, heal me, for my bones are troubled.
My soul also is greatly troubled; But You, O Lord—
    how long?" "I am weary with my groaning; All
    night I make my bed swim;
I drench my couch with my tears.
My eye wastes away because of grief."

Consider the real pain David expressed: *Lord, I need your mercy! I'm so tired of this sorrow. I'm so weak. My bones hurt; my heart hurts. How long is it going to feel like this? How long will I cry myself to sleep and wake up with ugly, swollen eyes? How long, Lord? How long?*

When you are grieving, it is good to openly acknowledge your sorrow and your pain – to say out loud that things have changed. That things aren't how they were. That you don't like it. That it's hard.

It's also healthy to allow your needs to be recognized by others as you experience grief. When you have experienced the death and loss of someone precious to you, everything's not okay, and you don't have to keep saying it is. You don't have to act like it is. Admit to others when you're hurting.

After acknowledging your grief, there are other steps that will help in the healing process.

Tell your story to others. Talk about your loved one, about your loss, and about your hope in Christ. When you are feeling distraught or hopeless, talk about that, too. Our need simply to talk to others is one of the reasons that a support group, or a circle of friends who have also walked through grief can be so important.

Commit to the journey that leads back to a full life, whether that journey is long or short. Although grief comes when the earthly life of a loved one is over, your life is not over. God still has a purpose for you in the land of the living. By His grace and through the healing He brings, the Lord will continue to use your life for His purpose and His glory.

Find ways to touch someone else's life. Don't wait until your grief has subsided to begin looking for specific ways to minister to others. As you serve others you will experience moments of joy, even during your season of grief.

More than anything else, trust God and cling to Him. Joy really does come in the morning, and until it does, He will carry you through the night.

THE TRANSFORMING EXPERIENCE OF GRIEF

In Psalm 30:11–12, David praises God for giving him joy following his grief:

> "You have turned for me my mourning into dancing;
>> You have put off my sackcloth and clothed me
>> with gladness,
> To the end that my glory may sing praise to You and
>> not be silent. O Lord my God, I will give thanks
>> to You forever."

I have watched men and women go through the pain of mourning and loss, so deeply hurt that I have frankly wondered if they would ever experience happiness again. Amazingly, God worked to restore them. Things are never the same after a profound loss, but things do improve. Joy and purpose come back to the surface of our lives as we trust God in our grief. God will bring you to the other side of your grief. But here are some things He will not do:

GOD WILL NOT ERASE YOUR GRIEF. You wouldn't want Him to. Grief is part of God's design for us to process our loss.

GOD WILL NOT PUSH THE FAST–FORWARD BUTTON ON YOUR GRIEF. One lady said, "I resent my grief. I wish God would give me a grief bypass." He won't.

But here is what God will do: He will transform your grief experience through the power of His Son, Jesus

Christ. The Bible says that God will turn our mourning into dancing.

The Hebrew word for *mourning* means wailing and crying out before God. The word for *dancing* doesn't mean a waltz or a line–dance; it means to dance around in circles spontaneously for joy.

You can't dance in circles for joy in the old drab sackcloth clothes of mourning! God will replace the black, uncomfortable mourning clothes with robes of gladness! And notice that we don't remove the sackcloth; He does! At the right time, He lifts the sackcloth off of us and replaces it with gladness, so that way down deep in our souls, we can sing of the glory and goodness of our God.

How can such a transformation occur? Only through the hope of eternal life in Jesus Christ.

King David suffered the death of his infant son after his sin and rebellion against God with Bathsheba. He grieved for that baby boy while he was sick, and begged God to heal his child. He didn't eat. He didn't sleep. David entered the depths of grief as he begged for God's mercy.

God didn't give David what he wanted. The child died. But David got up, washed his face, and began his life all over again.

When asked about it, David said this: "I can't bring him back to me, but I can go to him." David had the hope of eternal life in the Lord. Only believers in Jesus Christ can have that kind of hope that transforms grief into real and lasting joy.

It was the second Sunday of January 2007. It had been a really long day for me, preaching three services in the morning, and one that night. I was teaching a class the next morning in Lynchburg, Virginia, about three hours from my home. So, I was tired as I drove.

My cell phone rang, and it was my mother. "Stephen, grandmother's in the hospital." My grandmother, who I loved with all of my heart, had been diagnosed with cancer that fall. We knew that she only had months to live, but we thought we had more time than this. My mom told me she didn't think I needed to come; she just wanted me to know.

It wasn't long, however, before I got another call. "Stephen," my mother said, "I'm so sorry Grandmother just died." Well, mom and I cried and prayed on the phone. Then I turned my car around and drove to Greensboro, North Carolina, where I'm from.

I had taken off my coat and tie when I began my drive that afternoon. But when I got out of my car at the hospital, I put my tie back on, and slid my arms into my coat. I checked my hair and made sure I was good to see my grandmother for the last time.

In that hospital room, I sat next to her and took her hand in mine. Though her hand was still warm, I could feel the cold starting to seep into her fingers. I couldn't say anything. I just held her hand – the one she used to wave goodbye to me when I was a child. The hand she used to sew quilts that we still sleep under. I was my grandmother's only grandchild, and I loved her so much.

As I held her hand, I knew I was going to see her again. I'll squeeze her hand and she'll squeeze mine back. I knew for certain that day that I would see Grandmother again, because she loved Jesus, she's with Jesus now, and someday both she and I will be with Jesus together forever.

Jesus doesn't erase grief from our lives. But He does transform it into bright anticipation through His cross and His resurrection. The Bible gives us that assurance in Revelation 21:4:

> "And God shall wipe away every tear from their eyes; there shall be no more death. There shall be no more pain, for the former things have passed away."

You might just want to say those three words out loud: *No more death.* No more death! No more crying. No more pain.

Jesus willingly entered our grief. He took it with Him to the cross of Calvary, and He died to pay the price for your sin and my sin. And because He rose from the grave, He can give eternal, resurrection life to every person who trusts in Him. That promise transforms grief into hope.

As you read this, you may be dealing with overwhelming grief from a recent loss, or you may carry the chronic sorrow from a loss deep in your past. Today, the Lord wants to meet you in your grief. He wants to give you grace to alleviate the pain, and He wants to provide joy as you live. Take a moment to tell Him about your grief. Ask for His mercy. He alone can turn mourning into dancing!

Chapter 4
What? Me Worry?

"Do not worry."
MATTHEW 6:25

I want to confess a sin to you.

I struggled with this sin when I was a little boy. I was unable to conquer it as a teenager. As a young husband and pastor, I found myself wrestling with this sin every day. And even now, I occasionally struggle with it.

I don't think I've committed this sin today, but I have committed this sin within the past week.

It's a serious sin – so serious that Jesus Christ took time to address it and to warn against it.

Paul talked about this sin. The Psalms address this sin.

The sin I'm confessing to you today is worry. (If you were eager for me to confess something a little juicier, this is all you're getting!)

Worry is a sin. We consider worry as more of a weakness, but God calls worry wickedness. The same God who said, "You shall not kill," and "You shall not steal," and "You shall not bear false witness," and "You shall not commit adultery," also said with all the compassion of His heart, "Do not worry."

If you're one of those people who says, *I never worry about anything,* then I encourage you to share this book with someone who does worry. But you might want to hold on to it, just in case you need it.

It's hard to escape worry. One lady said to me, "You know, Pastor, I just don't really ever worry about anything. But I've got a daughter who worries about everything. I'm really worried about her."

We're going to look at what Jesus said about worry in the greatest sermon ever preached: the Sermon on the Mount. In that sermon, Jesus taught what it means to live a life of faith as a child of God. In the Sermon on the Mount, Jesus focuses like a laser on the issue of worry in our lives. These are the words of Jesus in Matthew 6:25–34:

> "Therefore I say to you, do not worry about your life, what you will eat or what you will drink; nor about your body, what you will put on. Is not life more than food and the body more than clothing?

Look at the birds of the air, for they neither sow nor reap nor gather into barns; yet your heavenly Father feeds them. Are you not of more value than they?

Which of you by worrying can add one cubit to his stature?

So why do you worry about clothing? Consider the lilies of the field, how they grow: they neither toil nor spin;

and yet I say to you that even Solomon in all his glory was not arrayed like one of these.

Now if God so clothes the grass of the field, which today is, and tomorrow is thrown into the oven, will He not much more clothe you, O you of little faith?

Therefore do not worry, saying, 'What shall we eat?' or 'What shall we drink?' or 'What shall we wear?'

For after all these things the Gentiles seek. For your heavenly Father knows that you need all these things.

But seek first the kingdom of God and His righteousness, and all these things shall be added to you.

Therefore do not worry about tomorrow, for tomorrow will worry about its own things. Sufficient for the day is its own trouble."

There you have it: Jesus said, not just once, but three times, *"Do not worry."* You'll find those words repeated in verses 25, 31, and 34 of Matthew 6. If Jesus tells us multiple times not to worry, then worry is a sin. That's bad news.

But there's also good news. Jesus died on the cross to pay for the sin of worry. He rose from the grave to give us victory over that sin. The beautiful message of Jesus is not just that you do not have to worry, but that He will give you His power day by day to deliver you from the sin of worry. He wants to take worry from you.

As we consider this teaching of Jesus, notice several reasons the Lord commands us not to worry.

WORRY REFUSES GOD'S SECURITY

In Matthew 6, verses 25 and 34, Jesus says,

> "Therefore I say to you, do not worry about your life, what you will eat or what you will drink; nor about your body, what you will put on. Is not life more than food and the body more than clothing?"
> "Therefore do not worry about tomorrow, for tomorrow will worry about its own things. Sufficient for the day is its own trouble."

Worry is a rejection of the security God wants for you. Worry is a big deal because it chokes our lives and strangles our faith.

The English word *worry* comes from an old Anglo–Saxon term that means to strangle. When a hunting dog finally catches a rabbit, grabs it by the neck and begins to shake the rabbit, the dog is said to *worry* the rabbit. If I were that rabbit, I would be worried, too.

Jesus says, *"Don't do that!"* Don't let worry strangle you! When believers choose worry, they refuse the security that God wants his children to enjoy.

In the verses we just read, Jesus names the things we worry about: our daily provisions, our physical well–being, and our future. Pretty much everything we worry about fits nicely in those three categories.

Jesus says not to worry about your life or your body. Who gave you life? God did. Who made your body? God did. So, if God gave you life, He's going to be faithful to sustain your life. And if God made your body, He's going to faithfully provide to take care of your body. Then, in verse 26, Jesus illustrates how God desires to take care of us:

> "Look at the birds of the air, for they neither sow nor reap nor gather into barns; yet your heavenly Father feeds them. Are you not of more value than they?"

Every day, all over the world, God provides food for the birds and other creatures He has made. Have you ever considered how much money it would take to feed all the wildlife in the world each day? No one in the world is rich enough to purchase all the food needed by all the wild animals in the world. But God feeds them every day.

The birds and other animals don't worry at all about where the next meal is coming from. Squirrels may look nervous and anxious, but even they know the food will be there. Beyond the wildlife that God feeds, Jesus points out the plant life that God clothes with beauty. Look in Matthew 6:28:

> "Why do you worry about clothing? Consider the lilies of the field, how they grow: they neither toil nor spin; and yet I say to you that even Solomon in all of his glory was not arrayed like one of these."

During his lifetime, King Solomon of Israel was the most powerful and wealthiest man on earth. He surely had a wardrobe fitting his position. And yet even his beautiful robes, crowns, rings, and shoes were no match for the beauty of the flowers of the field.

God takes care of the birds of the air and the flowers of the field because they belong to Him by virtue of creation. The Lord takes care of what He makes. But here's a wonderful thing to remember: If you have been saved by Jesus Christ, you not only belong to God by virtue of creation, but also by virtue of redemption. He made you in your mother's womb and breathed the breath of life into your lungs. And then He sacrificed His one and only Son upon the cross to redeem you with His own blood. Because of creation and redemption, he's committed to taking care of you. So why worry?

Continual worry is really a rejection of faith. When you ask God for His salvation, you ask in faith, believing. The Bible says that we are saved by faith when we realize our sin and confess it to God. We realize we cannot save ourselves, so we trust the work of Jesus Christ to save us. If you are saved, then you have trusted your very soul to Jesus.

And yet, many will trust their souls to Jesus, but not their bodies. Can we trust Jesus with our eternity, but not to help us pay our bills? Will you trust Jesus to take you to heaven when you die, but not to take care of your retirement years? Does that make sense to you? Of course not! Trusting Jesus for eternal salvation means also having faith in Him to care for you day by day.

Do this: Make a fist just as tight as you can. Squeeze so hard that your fingernails dig into your palm. Now hold it. Keep squeezing as hard as you can for as long as you can. For me, doing that becomes painful after a few moments. My hand goes numb.

That's what worry is. Worry is grabbing tightly to the details of your life, believing that no one else can take care of you. It's painful; it's paralyzing; and it can prevent you from doing anything else.

Now, open up that hand. Relax the muscles, and let go. That's what trusting the Lord is like. Saying no to worry means trusting God with everything you've held so tightly.

Your finances. Your kids. Your future. Your job and career. Your health. Psalm 37:3–4 says,

> "Trust in the Lord, and do good; dwell in the land, and
> feed on His faithfulness. Delight yourself also in
> the Lord, and He shall give you the desires of your
> heart."

Absolutely everything you need for salvation and for your physical life is found in Jesus. He will feed you with His faithfulness. He will sustain you with His goodness. So, trust God, and enjoy the security of His promise to care for your needs.

There's another reason Jesus commands us not to worry.

WORRY MISUSES ENERGY

Jesus asks a comical question in Matthew 6:27:

> "Which of you by worrying can add one cubit to his
> stature?"

With this question, Jesus creates an odd scenario. Here's a man who's worried about his height. If he were just taller, maybe eighteen inches or so, (the length of a cubit) he could achieve his dream of becoming a basketball superstar. He's fast. He's coordinated. He's got mad skills. But he's five feet six inches tall. He'll never be tall enough to be the next Michael Jordan or Steph Curry. And he worries, and worries, and worries about it.

Do you think he'll wake up one day and find that he's worried himself eighteen inches taller? No, that's silly!

In the same way, worry won't change the outcome of your situation. But it will prevent you from doing something so much better.

Years ago, when our son was a baby, our family was traveling from Mountain City, Tennessee to Bristol, Virginia. We were in an older car, and the route was mountainous. We came upon a sign that said:

SWITCHBACKS
NEXT 22 MILES

Neither Michele nor I knew what a switchback was, but we learned quickly as we climbed slowly up that mountain through a series of tight hairpin turns – just back and forth up the mountain, and then back and forth all the way back down on the other side.

After about eleven miles of switchbacks, our tired old car began to misbehave. The check engine light began to flash. I was in the passenger seat beginning to stew in my own worry. I thought, *"I haven't seen a house for eleven miles. I don't know if we're going to make it. The car's going to give out, and there's not even a shoulder to pull onto. Lord, my family's going to die right here on this mountain!*" I was flashing worry signals like a busy railroad crossing, breathing heavy, sighing, and rubbing my hands. Our baby son was asleep in the backseat, not a worry in his mind, but his dad was a basket case.

Michele looked at me. She said, "Stephen, what are you doing?" Oh, my wife knows me so well. I said, "I'm worrying." And she said, "Quit worrying and start praying." She gave me good advice.

After years of ministry, I have never once heard someone share a testimony about the positive power of worry. There's not one person who can say, *I worried and worried about my problem. I lost sleep, I bit my nails, and I got grumpy and irritated. And everything got better because I worried.* What you worried about may have never have come to pass, but not because you worried about it.

But there are plenty of testimonies from people who have encountered a difficulty and brought it to the Lord instead of worrying. They've said, *Lord, I can't handle this. I'm worried about this. I'm giving this to you because I can't take care of it. You take care of it.* And God has answered their prayers. God did what they could never have done.

Quit worrying and start praying! That's what Paul meant by his words in Philippians 4:6–7:

> "Be anxious for nothing, but in everything by prayer
> and supplication, with thanksgiving, let your re-
> quests be made known to God; and the peace of

God which surpasses all understanding, will guard
your hearts and minds through Christ Jesus."

On the side of that mountain, my wife knew prayer
was a reliable strategy.

So, we started praying. I prayed something like this:
"Lord, when we got this car, we dedicated it to You. So,
Lord, there seems to be a problem with Your car." And do
you know what? The check–engine light stopped flashing,
the car stopped lurching forward and going back, we made
it through all twenty–two miles of switchbacks, and then
home safely.

You only have so much energy. Don't waste it on
worry. Instead, invest it in prayer.

There's a third reason not to worry.

WORRY ABUSES OUR TESTIMONY

Jesus continues in Matthew 6:31–32:

> "Therefore do not worry, saying, 'What shall we eat?'
>   or 'What shall we drink?' or 'What shall we wear?'
> For after all these things the Gentiles seek."

Here, Jesus draws a distinction between Gentiles and
Jews. Gentiles were pagans, separated from God's promises. The Jews were God's own special people. The Lord
was telling His listeners – all Jews – that when they worried

about the daily needs of life, they were acting just like the godless Gentiles. In our context, as believers, Jesus is saying this: When we, God's saved people, worry about the details of our lives – What will I eat? What will I drink? What will I wear? How we'll ever make it through? – we're not acting like saved people; we're acting like lost people.

If you have been bold enough to identify as a follower of Jesus Christ, then people in your family, your community and your workplace are watching.

They're skeptical, not yet convinced that your faith in Jesus Christ makes a real difference in your life. They don't just want to see you going to church on Sunday. That, in itself, will not impress them. They're really not interested in your rituals or your spiritual language. They want to know if you're really trusting God, day by day.

If you confront the issues of life with the same worry and anxiety that they do, they'll notice that as well. A believer's testimony can be terribly damaged by living a worry–filled life.

But when unbelievers see you face problems, concerns, heartaches, and the stresses of life with faith that God will take care of it, that's proof of a genuine transformation that Jesus has accomplished in your life.

I had just finished preaching a message on breaking free from worry at a church one Sunday. After the services were over, a woman named Liz came up to talk with me. She shared the beautiful story about how she became a Christian. Liz grew up in a home that was nominally Christian. Her family claimed a denominational affiliation, but didn't believe in Jesus, or in God, or in the Bible.

When Liz became an adult, she moved to a new city. In her new workplace she met a number of believers, one in particular caught Liz's attention. This woman was never obnoxious, never pushy, but she took every opportunity to talk to Liz about Jesus. She invited Liz to church.

Liz truly enjoyed the lady's company and appreciated her friendship. But she politely refused the invitations, insisting that she really was fine and didn't need religion.

Then Liz's life was turned upside down. Her mother-in-law became ill and had to be put into a nursing home. Her father began to experience dementia and no longer recognized her. Financial troubles set in, making it difficult to pay the mortgage. Their teenage daughter ran wild. Liz was at a loss for what to do.

Worry and anxiety moved in like squatters, taking over Liz's heart and mind.

But Liz knew that her friend at work was also going through many of the same difficulties: financial trouble, issues with aging parents, rebellious teenagers. Yet, every day she came to work with a deep sense of peace. Instead of worrying and complaining about her own issues, she asked Liz regularly how she could pray for her.

Finally, Liz asked her friend, "How are you managing all this so well? What do you have that I don't?" Her friend smiled and answered, "Liz, it's not what I've got; it's Who I've got. His name is Jesus."

Liz placed her faith in Jesus Christ. She led her family to Jesus. And all of this happened because of a believer who lived a life of faith instead of worry.

What do onlookers see in your life? When your family and neighbors know you are facing difficulty, what response do they see and hear in you? What about your kids? Do they hear late–night conversations laced with anxiety, or do they hear late–night prayers filled with faith?

Don't let worry make your testimony for Jesus Christ ineffective. Instead, let faith protect it so that others will be drawn to your Helper – Jesus.

Jesus offers a final reason not to worry.

Worry Confuses Our Priorities

The words of Jesus in Matthew 6:33 are often quoted:

> "But seek first the kingdom of God and His righteous-
> ness, and all these things shall be added to you."

I learned Matthew 6:33 by singing a little chorus with those words, from the King James. Whatever translation is used, most of the time when people quote Matthew 6:33, they leave out the first word, *But*.

That word is so very important! The word *but* here means instead of. Jesus is saying, "Instead of worrying, seek first the kingdom of God and His righteousness." Rather than worrying about all of those things that God knows you need and has promised to provide, the number one priority in your life should be this: seeking God's kingdom. We seek God's kingdom by striving to make Jesus Christ the King and Lord of every part of our lives. It means to make righteous living that pleases God our highest priority.

Mark Jones, the kid's pastor at Quail Springs Baptist church where I serve, presents the gospel to children by calling on boys and girls to "make Jesus the boss of your life." That's a really helpful description of what it means to seek God's kingdom. Seeking His kingdom means He's the Boss!

There's a promise for obeying that command: "And all these things will be added to you." Don't miss that.

When you make Jesus your boss, He will provide all the things you really need in your life. What things? The things you probably tend to worry about! Your money. Your job. Your kids. Your health. Your future. Does that mean that all of your problems will go away if you trust Jesus? No; it does mean that when you entrust them to His care, He will take care of you.

On the way home from church, Jack was riding in the back seat of his parents' car. His dad glanced in the rearview mirror and caught sight of Jack, who seemed to be having a hard time with something. He was fidgety and squirmed in his seat. "Hey buddy, what's the matter?" his dad asked.

Jack responded, "I'm worried, Dad. I've made bad grades on all my math tests this semester. Dad, I've worked hard, but I'm afraid I'm going to fail. I'm nervous every day when I go to school." He paused. "Dad, that song we sang in church today – *God Will Take Care of You.* Dad, is that true?"

Jack's dad said, "Yes, son, God will take care of you. You tell Him what You need, and you study and do your best. Stop worrying, because God will take care of you in that math class."

The next day, the dad arrived at work. Before he even got to his desk, here came his boss. "John, your numbers were less than stellar last month. You're just not producing what we need. We'll give it one more month, John, and if your numbers haven't improved, well, John, you need to look for another job."

John's mind raced back to his conversation with his son. He thought about his daughter who needed braces; about another son starting college; about the house payment. He began to pray. Then he called his pastor. "Pastor, that song we sang yesterday – *God Will Take Care of You.* Pastor, is that really true?"

The pastor said, "Oh yes, John, it's true. I don't know what you're going through, but it's true, John. God will take care of you. Stop worrying, and keep praying. You can trust God, John. He'll take care of all you need."

The pastor hung up the phone. And his mind jumped to the rumblings in the church. There were so many complaints. Ministry felt like trying to push a wagon full of concrete uphill. He was seeing little progress, and he was worried. He fell to his knees and cried out, "Lord! You know what they're saying. And that song we sang yesterday – *God Will Take Care of You*." Lord, is that true? Will you really take care of me?" And it was as though the Holy Spirit laid His hand firmly upon the pastor's shoulder and said, "Yes, son. You can stop worrying. I will take care of you."

God knows every worrisome detail of your life. Jesus Christ, through His Word, says to you right now, "Do not worry. I died on the cross to pay the full price for all of your sin, including your worry. I rose from the grave to give you victory over every sin, including worry. So let go of your worry, trust Me. I will take care of you."

Chapter 5
Alone in a Crowd

"I cry out to the Lord with my voice; With my voice to the
Lord I make my supplication.
I pour out my complaint before Him; I declare before Him
my trouble. When my spirit was overwhelmed within
me, Then You knew my path.
In the way in which I walk
They have secretly set a snare for me.
Look on my right hand and see,
For there is no one who acknowledges me; Refuge has failed
me; No one cares for my soul.
I cried out to You, O Lord:
I said, "You are my refuge,
My portion in the land of the living.
Attend to my cry,
For I am brought very low;
Deliver me from my persecutors, For they are stronger than I.

Bring my soul out of prison,
That I may praise Your name;
The righteous shall surround me,
For You shall deal bountifully with me."

PSALM 142:1–7

———————————

Almost eight billion people. That's the population of planet earth. More than at any time in history.

Advances in technology have matched the growth in population so that we are more connected than ever before. Statistics tell us …

» In 2021, there are 4.66 billion active internet users.

» The number of connected cell phones is expected to reach more than 17 billion by 2024– twice as many phones as people.

» In 2021 there are 4.2 billion active social media users.

Anyone anywhere in the world could text a message to me right now and I'd have it within seconds. Most everybody I know has a cell phone. Every day, we use technology we only saw on the *The Jetsons* when we were growing up. We have the resources to be better connected than ever before. And yet …

A man sits alone in a nursing home, wondering why his son who lives just across town doesn't call. He hasn't visited in six months, and he probably won't visit this month either. He's lonely.

In a four-bedroom house, a mom and dad have been consumed with kid-life for nineteen years. And now the nest is empty, and only the memory of children's voices echo in the hallway. They feel alone.

An eighteen-year-old college student with a thousand "friends" on social media can never find someone to eat with. Night after night she pops in a microwave meal, plops in front of the TV, and zones out until she can't keep her eyes open. That's the routine. She's alone.

Twenty-five percent of Americans do not have a close friend: no confidant, no sounding board, no one to share the stuff of life with. We have become increasingly connected, but strangely lonely.

David wrote Psalm 142 from inside a cave. He was being hunted down by his enemies and had fled into the cave for refuge. If you're hiding in a cave, you're probably pretty lonesome. And I use the word *lonesome* intentionally, because it seems even lonelier that the word *lonely*. Lonely is bad; lonesome is worse. Hank Williams sang, famously, *"I'm so lonesome I could cry."* But for the believer, even in our loneliest hours, God is working. What does God do when you are lonely?

GOD NEVER STOPS LISTENING

In the first two verses of Psalm 142, David wrote,

> "I cry out to the Lord with my voice; With my voice to
>   the Lord I make my supplication.
> I pour out my complaint before Him;
> I declare before Him my trouble."

Have you ever cried aloud to God? I have many times, and I'm in good company. David felt his loneliness so keenly that he cried out loud. That means that he wailed in pain and anguish: *I'm hurting Lord! Help me!*

He pleaded with God for mercy. His cry was desperate.

David also poured out his complaints before God. Like blood gushing from an open wound, he poured out his heartache before the Lord.

And then, he declared to the Lord his trouble. He told God all he was going through. Did the Lord already know? Yes, but there is something about saying it out loud.

Notice that all of the verbs used here – *cry, make my supplication, pour out, declare my trouble* – are present tense, which tells us that David didn't just do this once; he did it over and over and over. Standing at the mouth of that cave, you would have heard a man of strong faith and trust in God screaming to God, crying to God, wailing to God: "*Lord, it's me, David!*

Do you see me here in this cave? Lord, I'm hurting! Lord, I'm under attack! And I feel so all alone."

In the South, sometimes a frustrated parent will say to a complaining child, *"Quitcherbellyachin!"* But God didn't do that with David. He never stopped listening to David's complaints. He didn't get tired of hearing it. As long as David was calling out, God continued to listen. God never stops listening.

But sometimes we stop talking. We give up on telling God our needs, our pains, and our loneliness. I think we do that because we don't fully understand the purpose and the power of prayer.

Many Christians treat prayer like a spare tire for their car. When you purchase a car, you make sure it has a spare inflated and ready in case you have a flat. And it's locked in the well, where it's out of sight, out of mind. Then you have a flat. Maybe you can't remember where the spare is, so you grab the owner's manual to help you find it. When you do find it, you're not quite sure how to get to it, or how to use the weird jack that came with the car. The spare is always there, but you really don't rely on it, or think about it, or know how to use it.

Prayer isn't a spare tire for your life. It shouldn't be your last resort when you get to your wit's end. Instead, prayer should be more like the steering wheel of your car that steers your faith in the right direction.

Or like the engine that moves you along. Or like your transmission that gets things in gear. Prayer is the heart of the Christian life and keeps us connected to our heavenly Father. When we pray, He's always listening. When we're the loneliest, we should be talking to God the most.

David described his pattern of prayer in Psalm 55:17:

> "Evening, morning and at noon I will pray, and cry aloud."

Indeed, David may have had a morning prayer time, a noon prayer time, and an evening prayer time. What he is describing here, however, is far more comprehensive than that. David is saying that prayer is an all–day conversation– a constant communication between him and God. Prayer is not a one– way conversation. God participates. He listens.

Perhaps you feel that your loneliness isn't something significant enough to bother God with. I want to remind you: there are no insignificant needs.

A lady said to her pastor, "Reverend, I only bring the big things to God. I don't ask Him about the small things." Her pastor replied wisely, "Sister, everything you bring to God is small to Him."

Whether your need seems big or small, it's all small to God. There's nothing too difficult to Him. He is always available. He can hear your voice out of the millions of voices crying to Him all day, every day. Your voice is as important as any of the others. He sees your heart, and He hears every prayer. He is always listening.

GOD NEVER STOPS CARING

In Psalm 142:3, David says,

> "When my spirit was overwhelmed within me, then
> You knew my path. In the way in which I walk."

David's spirit was fainting. He didn't think he could keep going. He was overwhelmed. But God knew David's path.

Your path includes every aspect of your life – your past, your present, and your future. At every point along your path, God knows and cares. He knows your regrets and the guilt that springs from your past. He knows the loneliness, frustration, and emptiness you face right now. He knows your apprehensions about the future. When your life feels shattered in a million pieces, God cares.

Michele and I had been working on a photo collage that we intended to hang in my office. It was a joyful, but painstaking process.

We went through scores of recent digital photos of our family, trying to select the eight that we most loved to place in the collage. We printed the photos, and cut them carefully. Then we removed the back from the frame and began to place the pictures. We made sure they were straight and carefully taped them to the glass.

When all the photos were in place, we replaced the back of the frame, making sure it was fastened tightly. Michele took a cloth and made sure the glass was clean and sparkling.

It was beautiful and showed off memories of things we'd done together as a family for the past couple of years.

We knew exactly where the collage was to hang in my office. The picture hangers were already in place. So, I headed across the room with the frame to hang the collage on the wall. I was holding it by the cord hanger, and as I walked, that cord broke in two. Our beautiful family collage fell to the floor and shattered.

We hadn't seen that coming. We picked up the pieces and threw them in the garbage. We went home so disappointed.

That's the way the path of your life can go. Hard things happen, and you didn't anticipate the loneliness and the hurt you feel. But here you are, smack dab in the middle of it, and it feels like not one soul cares.

One of the loneliest verses in the Bible is Psalm 143:4:

"Look on my right hand and see,
For there is no one who acknowledges me;
Refuge has failed me;
No one cares for my soul."

A different translation says it this way: "There's not even one person who knows my name."

Have you ever felt like that? Nobody cares for my soul. No one asks about me. No one calls me. Nobody's looking for me. Nobody comes to visit. Nobody cares.

Jesus cares. He never stops caring for you. He never stops caring for others.

In fact, we are the instruments He wants to use to care for others in His name.

The way we can best care for the souls of people is to share the love of Jesus Christ with them. I'm so glad that someone cared for my soul enough to share the good news of salvation with me. And I'm even more glad that Jesus cared for my soul enough that He would go to the cross of Calvary and pay the price with His own precious blood for my soul. He didn't stop one step shy of the cross because He cares for you, and He cares for others. He never stops. And because He never stops caring, He never, ever forsakes us.

Psalm 37:25 says,

"I have been young and now I am old; yet I have never seen the righteous forsaken, nor his descendants begging for bread."

Jesus never, ever forsakes the righteous. He never leaves them alone. He never stops caring.

GOD NEVER STOPS WORKING

David says in verse 5 of Psalm 142,

> "I cried out to You, O Lord:
> I said, 'You are my refuge,
> My portion in the land of the living.'"

God works on our behalf when we are lonely. David called God his refuge. That means God was David's hiding place; his shelter; his fortress; and his place of safety. David didn't say, *"This cave is my refuge."* No. God Himself was David's refuge. God was working to protect David.

God was also David's portion. David knew that as long as he had God, then he had everything he needed, including deliverance.

As the Psalm continues, David says in verses 6 and 7,

> "Attend to my cry, for I am brought very low; deliver
>   me from my persecutors, for they are stronger than
>   I. Bring my soul out of prison, That I may praise
>   Your name."

Remember, David was being pursued by wicked King Saul. Saul had both the military power and the manpower to hunt David down. Saul's forces were stronger than David by a long shot; but God was working to deliver David and set him free from the grasp of Saul and his men.

David was confident that God would set him free. As a result, he was preparing his heart to praise the one who cared for him. He was getting ready to worship the one he knew would deliver him. He knew God would deal bountifully with him to bless, protect, provide, and deliver him from his enemies.

David hadn't seen it yet, but he knew it was coming because He knew his God cared for him, even when He was silent.

Someone made this observation to me once, and I'll never forget it. They said, "When I was in school, I don't remember the teacher ever talking when she was giving a test."

When we go through times of testing, sometimes the Lord just doesn't say a whole lot. He stands in the back of the room where you can't see Him. And you wonder, *Is He here? I don't see anything happening.* Rest assured that God has never left you and He never will, because He never stops caring for you.

Corrie ten Boom, along with her family were used by God to hide many Jewish families in their home during the Holocaust. They were arrested by the Nazis and sent to horrific concentration camps. Many of Corrie's family, including her precious sister, died in those camps. Corrie herself was placed in solitary confinement for four months.

Inside that tiny, nasty cell, Corrie could hear the screams of other prisoners being tortured. She was frightened, and she was so very lonely. One day she cried out and said, "Lord, I cannot make it! I can't do this! I'm all alone, and my faith is so weak!"

As Corrie looked down through her tears, she saw an ant scooting across the floor toward a puddle of water. As soon as the ant's feet touched the water, he turned and scurried back to his hole.

Corrie felt the Lord speak to her. He said, "Corrie, do you see how that ant came out from his hiding place? And when his feet touched the water, he ran back to his hiding place? Corrie, I am your hiding place. Don't look at how weak your faith is. Don't look at how horrible your circumstances are. You look at Me; run to Me. And just as that ant disappeared into its hiding place, you run to me. I will protect you."

There, in that lonely place, Corrie ten Boom trusted God, and He brought her through.

You may feel like the loneliest person on earth. You feel weak in your faith, and that you won't make it through circumstances that are beyond your control. But if you know Jesus Christ as your Savior, you are never alone.

Jesus hung on the cross of Calvary for six grueling hours. And before He died, He cried to God,

"My God! My God! Why have you forsaken Me!"

MATTHEW 27:46

In those moments on the cross, Jesus Christ was the loneliest person in the entire universe, for all of history. It is beyond my understanding how the eternal Father could forsake His eternal Son. But there on that awful cross, Jesus Christ bore in His body all of our sin, all of our griefs, all of our sorrow, all of our loneliness, and all of our forsakenness. He was forsaken by God so that you don't have to be.

Jesus Himself said,

"I will never leave you nor forsake you."

HEBREWS 13:5

When you are all alone, God never stops listening. He never stops caring. He never stops working. And He will never, no never, forsake you.

Chapter 6

Crimes and Misdemeanors

Psalm 32

*Blessed is he whose transgression is forgiven, Whose sin is
 covered.*

*Blessed is the man to whom the LORD does not impute
 iniquity,
And in whose spirit there is no deceit.*

*When I kept silent, my bones grew old
Through my groaning all the day long.
For day and night Your hand was heavy upon me;
My vitality was turned into the drought of summer. Selah
I acknowledged my sin to You,
And my iniquity I have not hidden.
I said, "I will confess my transgressions to the LORD,"*

And You forgave the iniquity of my sin. Selah

For this cause everyone who is godly shall pray to You
In a time when You may be found; Surely in a flood of
  great waters
They shall not come near him.
You are my hiding place;
You shall preserve me from trouble;
You shall surround me with songs of deliverance. Selah

I will instruct you and teach you in the way you should go;
I will guide you with My eye.
Do not be like the horse or like the mule,
Which have no understanding,
Which must be harnessed with bit and bridle, Else they will
  not come near you.

Many sorrows shall be to the wicked;
But he who trusts in the LORD, mercy shall surround him.
Be glad in the LORD and rejoice, you righteous; And shout
  for joy, all you upright in heart!

———

The year was 1937. New London High School had been built in oil–rich London, Texas, just a few years earlier. It was a beautiful school. To save money heating the building, the school board had decided to capture the waste natural gas produced by a nearby gasoline refinery. It would be syphoned from the refinery to the high school, and used to heat the building.

At 3:17 p.m. on March 18, with just minutes left in the school day and more than 500 students and teachers inside the building, a sudden and catastrophic explosion leveled most of what had been the wealthiest rural school in the nation.

Natural gas in its pure state is odorless. No one detected that it had been leaking, and had pooled inside the walls and the basement. Someone plugged in an electrical woodshop sander, it caused a spark, and the gas was ignited without warning.

Two hundred ninety–three people died in the explosion. Every family in London, Texas, lost someone that day. The whole town was devastated. The only positive thing that came from the tragedy was that the government mandated the addition of an odor to natural gas that makes it easily detectable.[2]

All natural gas now has a pungent odor that kind of stings the hairs in your nose. It stinks, like rotten eggs, but it helps prevent great devastation.

God has added something to your heart so that you know when things are not right with Him. Guilt is that twinge of conscience, the heaviness that we feel when we know we've done something that doesn't please God.

Is guilt bad, or is guilt good? There is a bad guilt. We might call it misplaced guilt. If you feel guilty for something

---

2   https://www.aoghs.org/oil–almanac/new–london–texas–school– explosion/

you've never done; if you feel guilty but you have no idea what your sin is; if you've confessed a sin and repented, God has forgiven you, but you still feel guilty – those are all examples of misplaced guilt. God doesn't want you to carry the burden of misplaced guilt.

But good guilt, like the unpleasant odor in natural gas, is a warning that something isn't right between you and God. Good guilt comes from God as a result of committing sin. But God doesn't want you to carry good guilt forever! He wants to remove the heaviness of guilt from our lives so we can enjoy fellowship with Him again. In Psalm 32, David describes several ways God can deal graciously and redemptively with our guilt.

GOD CARRIES AWAY OUR TRANSGRESSIONS

Psalm 32:1 begins with a blessing:

"Blessed is he whose transgression is forgiven."

David had sinned grievously. He had experienced tremendously heavy guilt. But at the time when he wrote this Psalm, he was on the other side of that experience. He had confessed his sin and had been made right with God. Experientially, David could say, *I'm blessed – I'm happy – because my sin is forgiven.*

The Hebrew word for *transgression* means rebellion. What did David know of rebellion? He had lived for the Lord all of His life. The Bible calls David *a man after God's own heart.* He was the King of Israel. He was famous. He was a great military man. He loved the Lord, and he loved his people. He was a reputable man, an ethical man.

But when David was around fifty years old, he got spiritually lazy and let his guard down. And the devil came knocking on the door of David's heart. You can read the story in 2 Samuel, chapter 11, but here's what happened.

Think spring training. It was the time of year when kings were supposed to go to war. But David decided that this year, he didn't need to join the team on the field. He stayed home in Jerusalem.

One night David became restless. Maybe he was bored. Maybe he had no one to hang out with. He got up from his bed and went to the rooftop of his house. As he looked out over the city, he saw a beautiful woman bathing on her rooftop. Her name was Bathsheba.

Now, David should have turned his eyes away. He should have changed the channel and watched something else, but he didn't. Instead, he asked his servant about her, and learned that she was married to Uriah, one of David's trusted soldiers who was away in the war.

What a perfect opportunity! David was king, so he could have whatever he wanted. Uriah was away. It was nighttime. Who would know? David sent for Bathsheba. He slept with her, and then sent her back to her house. From what we read in the biblical narrative, David seemed to have treated the whole abysmal event as though it was no big deal. But in a few weeks, David received this message from Bathsheba: "*I'm pregnant.*"

This certainly wasn't part of David's plan. So, he devised a plan to make Uriah think the child was his. He called Uriah home for a couple of days of R&R. Uriah walked in. David rushed to meet him. "Hey, Uriah! Good to see you, man! How's the war? You guys taking care of business? You know, I really appreciate you so much. I just want you to go home tonight and enjoy some time with your wife."

But Uriah's sense of duty and honor wouldn't allow it. He said to David, "No sir, I can't do that. My fellow soldiers are out on the battlefield. The ark of the covenant of God is out on the battlefield. I can't sleep in my house while they're out there. That wouldn't be right." So, Uriah slept on David's doorstep.

David tried again the next day. He wined and dined Uriah. When Uriah became drunk, he helped him out the door and pointed him toward home. But Uriah's sense of honor was so strong that even in his drunken state, he would not acquiesce to David's plan.

David was desperate. He wrote a letter to Uriah's commander, and it said, "I want you to put Uriah on the front line of the battle, and leave him there alone." He handed Uriah the letter and sent him to deliver it to his commander. The commander obeyed David's directive. Uriah died in the heat of battle.

David called for Bathsheba and married her. From David's perspective, problem solved.

Can you imagine a man like David doing a thing such as what I have just described? This is the same David who wrote, "The Lord is my shepherd; I shall not want. Surely goodness and mercy will follow me all the days of my life." In the space of only a few months, the same man God had used so mightily in the past had become a slacker, a coveter, an adulterer, a thief, a liar, a schemer, and a murderer.

Pretty terrible, huh? Yes, David's sin was horrible. David experienced tremendous guilt. It made him depressed and physically ill. But it drove him back to God. He confessed his sin and received God's forgiveness. That's why he could say,

> "Blessed is he whose transgression [whose rebellion] is
> forgiven"
>
> PSALM 32:1

Forgiven is one of the most beautiful words in all the Bible. It literally means to lift up and carry away.

Every Wednesday night, Michele collects all the little plastic bags in all the wastebaskets in our house carries them to the big trash bag. Then she ties up the big trash bag, hands it to me, and says, "Please take this out."

So, I take the trash outside to the garbage can. Then, I wheel the garbage can to the end of our driveway and leave it overnight.

Sometime before the sun comes up, sanitation workers come by and take all of our garbage away. I don't know where they take it. All I know is that when I go outside, it's gone. I can't find it. I can't even smell it anymore.

You know, the sanitation workers have never knocked on my front door to ask if I have any trash that needs to be taken away. I do my part, and they do their part. I take it to the curb, and they take it away. That's how it works.

But God is so much more gracious. He not only takes the trash away, but He comes knocking on the door of your life and says, "Hey, you got any garbage in there? I smell something in there you need to get rid of." That's what guilt is. Guilt is God saying, "You've got garbage in there. Don't you want to do something about that?"

But you've got to do your part. You've got to take out the trash through confession of your sin, which is simply agreeing with God; saying, "*Yes, there is trash in my life. I've done this; I've sinned; I've rebelled; I've transgressed.*" Maybe your sin seems small, like you just need a little grocery bag to carry it out. Or maybe you feel your sin would better fit into a forty–gallon trash bag. But when guilt says, "You've got sin in your life," you should simply agree with God, and say, "You're right, Lord. This is what I've done. I'm sorry, and I don't want this anymore. Would you take this away?" And then, through the wonderful grace of Jesus Christ, He carries it away.

The waste management people take my trash some-where in my county. But the Bible says that God removes our sin from us as far as the east is from the west, and that he buries it in the depths of the sea. Praise God! He carries away our guilt and our transgressions so far away, that they can never come back.

GOD COVERS OUR SIN

The first part of Psalm 32 verse 1 says,

"Blessed is he whose sin is covered."

Not only does God carry our sins far away from us; He covers the stain of our sin.

The word *covered* means concealed or hidden. It can't be seen anymore. The word *sin* means anything that comes short of God's expectations for us. It's really an athletic term.

If you watch a Sunday afternoon golf tournament on television, you'll see this: A player putts from sixty feet, or sometimes from just two feet. The ball rolls toward the hole, and then stops an inch short. It might even have stopped a foot short. Or it might have swung left or right of the hole and missed badly. Whether the putt comes up short or goes the wrong direction, the result is the same. The golfer missed his target. He missed his goal.

We've all fallen short of God's glory. It's the goal, but we'll never hit it. We will always fall short; we sin. And our sin leaves a stain on our lives like spaghetti sauce on a white carpet. It's impossible to cover up.

Psalm 28:13 testifies to the futility of trying to conceal your own sin:

"He who covers his sin will not prosper. But whoever confesses and forsakes them will have mercy."

Several years ago, we had a stain on our kitchen ceiling where some water had leaked from the upstairs bathtub. Every time you looked up there it was – an ugly discolored spot. Everything else in the kitchen looked great, but that stain just made the whole thing look dirty.

So, I painted over the stain. It looked great. But when the paint had dried, the stain was still there, ugly as ever. So, I applied a second coat of paint. Looked great. Until the paint dried. I tried a few more times with the same result. I did not prosper as I tried to cover that stain!

Sometimes we may try to escape the guilt of our sin by numbing our minds with drugs or alcohol. But the guilt seeps through. We still sense the reality of our sin, and our attempt to cover things up only makes the situation worse. We may try to paint over the stain of our sin with things like work, or entertainment, or even religion. None of that will remove the stain and guilt of your sin.

Sometimes we shift blame for our sin onto something or someone else, or we refuse to call what God says is sin, sin. We say,

> *"This really isn't my fault. It's because my mom or dad did this or that."*
> *"This isn't sin. This is who I am. I was born this way."*
> *"I love this person. It just feels so right."*

Blame–shifting won't cover your sin–stain. Refusing to acknowledge sin won't lift the stain.

You will never succeed in trying to cover your own sin.

For a long time, David tried to conceal his sin. He lied. He murdered. He married Bathsheba. He showed kindness to her. But none of his attempts cleared him of his guilt. The rest of his life may have looked really good, but every time he looked at himself, there was that big ugly stain. His whole life was dirty.

Back to my kitchen ceiling. After all of my unsuccessful attempts to clean up my ceiling, we called a professional, who had the right stuff, the right materials, and the right methods so that he could cover the stain. When he was done, our ceiling looked as good as new.

In a much better way, God covers our sin. He paints over our sin with the blood of His own Son, Jesus Christ. The stain of your sin can never soak through the blood of Jesus. It never requires a second coat.

God completely covers our sin.

GOD CLEARS OUR NAME

David continues in Psalm 32:2:

> "Blessed is the man to whom the Lord does not impute iniquity."

You probably have a credit card in your wallet or purse. With that card, you can buy a lot of things and not have to pay for them – for thirty days. Then the fun's over.

When your credit card statement comes, every purchase you made the previous month is itemized. It's really clear what you bought, and what you owe. The debt is *imputed* to you.

You've got three options. You could bury that bill in the back yard and try to cover it up like we talked about, but almost magically, another bill will come next month. And not only will you still owe last month's debt, but there will be more and more and more charges. You'll never be able to just forget about it.

A second option is to make the minimum payment every month. That will keep the credit card company satisfied temporarily. But making the minimum payment doesn't satisfy the debt. The credit card company will continue to contact you monthly looking for you to pay.

But the third option is, by far, the best. You can pay the debt in full. Then it will no longer be hanging over your head, no one will continually demand payment, and it won't be a threat to your future.

Our sin–debts are the same. We can't cover them; they keep coming back up. Making the minimum payment of trying to do better will perhaps relieve you a little for today, but your debt to God will just continue to grow. You'll never pay it off, because you don't have the resources.

We are all spiritually bankrupt. No man is rich enough to be able to pay his own sin–debt. And when you die, there will be a demand for payment in full. Those who cannot pay will be cast into an eternal debtor's prison called Hell.

But Jesus Christ paid the full price to clear your sin–debt when He died on the cross! On the cross, He wrote *"paid in full"* across the list of debts you owe!

Jesus has paid for your sin, and paid in full.

If the devil comes and says, "Hey, you did so and so back when you were young; you need to pay for that," Jesus steps in and says, "Nope; that bill's been paid." Or if Satan says, "I found this invoice with your name on it. It's pretty big; you owe for that!" Jesus steps in and shows His nail–scarred hands and feet and says, "No, Satan, you're mistaken. I paid that debt Myself a long time ago."

I love the words to this old song[3]:

> *There was a time on earth, when in the book of heaven*
> *An old account was standing of sins yet unforgiven.*
> *My name was at the top and many things below,*
> > *But I went to the Master and settled long ago.*
> *Long ago, down on my knees; long ago, I settled it all.*
> > *Yes, the old account was settled long ago.*
> *And my record's clear today, for He washed my sins*
> *away*
> > *When the old account was settled long ago.*

Someone has said that when Jesus died on the cross, it was as though He wrote a check that pays the price for every sin you have ever committed, past, present, and future.

---

3   "An Old Account Settled," F. M. Graham, 1951, Public Domain.

And when the debt is paid in full, it is covered, never to be resubmitted for payment.

I used to carpool with a guy who had just bought a used car. Or, as he called it, a certified, pre–owned vehicle! The car was beautiful and ran great. But one of the dashboard lights flashed constantly. This went on for weeks.

One morning when he picked me up, I couldn't see the light flashing. I said, "Hey, you got your car fixed." He said, "Look closer." The light was still flashing, but he had covered it with a piece of black tape. Whatever the problem was, it was still there.

Guilt is a flashing light that says, *"Something's wrong that you need to take care of."* Instead, bring your guilt to Jesus and He'll fix the problem that's causing your guilt. He'll carry your guilt away. He'll cover the sin. And He'll clear your name through His own blood.

Chapter 7
What's Your Problem?

I have a friend who sees himself as a problem solver, with good reason. He spent his professional career as a pediatric dentist, traveling from place to place to provide dental care for children, many of whom came from underprivileged or impoverished families. A good number of these kids had neglected to care for their teeth. Others were born with serious dental problems that had never been corrected, and that required immediate treatment.

My dentist friend would arrive on the scene armed with his training and his experience in diagnosing and treating children. Beyond that, he came feeling a moral and ethical duty to help. And so, for years, he relentlessly solved problems. He helped children with dental issues they keenly felt, such as severe toothaches. He also worked to solve problems the children couldn't see or didn't feel, but would lead to serious issues later on if unaddressed.

My friend lived by this conviction: If you see a problem, and you can correct a problem, compassion says that you must seek to solve the problem. That's what God has done for us through His Son, Jesus.

In this book, we have seen how God works graciously in our lives to solve our greatest problems. With mercy and compassion, He heals our hidden hurts. Some are hurts that we feel acutely but choose to keep hidden. We may not tell anyone about the fears that haunt us in the middle of the night, the loneliness we mask with a cheerful disposition, or the deep–seated anger we work so hard to suppress in public. Other types of pain in our lives may be hidden even from ourselves. The pain of grief and loss or the weight of guilt can be buried so deeply that we are unaware of their effects on us, but the hurt is still very real, and still harmful.

God knows us perfectly. He can see every problem in our lives, even the ones we do not feel. Even more wonderfully, God has provided the solution to the problem of brokenness in our lives and separation from God. The ultimate cure for every hidden hurt comes through God's plan for redemption and salvation in Jesus Christ.

Your greatest problem is your own sinfulness.

Sin causes us to be spiritually dead. In Ephesians 2:1, the Bible says we are "dead in trespasses and sins." Sin is anything we say, do, or think that does not please God. It's also when we fail to do the things that please God. Most people understand that they have sinned and made mistakes. After all, nobody is perfect. What we often do not understand, however, is that our sin offends God deeply, breaking His heart and separating us from Him. Isaiah 59:2 says,

> "Your iniquities have separated you from your God;
>   And your sins have hidden His face from you."

Sin is our biggest problem because it keeps us from truly knowing God and spending eternity with Him. Sin is a problem that we cannot solve on our own. Even if we do a lot of good, noble things, those good things will not make up for our sin. If we perform all kinds of religious rituals and ceremonies, religion will not erase our sin. If we try to be moral and ethical in all we do, we still come up short because we are sinners at heart. In Isaiah 64:6, God tells us that our best efforts are still insufficient to please Him and overcome our sin:

> "We are all like an unclean thing,
> And all our righteousnesses are like filthy rags;
> We all fade as a leaf,
> And our iniquities, like the wind,
> Have taken us away."

Because God loves us, He has made the way to solve the problem of our sin. God sent Jesus, His Son, to be born as a baby, to live a perfect life as a man, and then to die in our place for our sins. The beautiful words of John 3:16 tell us,

> "For God so loved the world that He gave His only be-
> gotten Son, that whoever believes in Him should
> not perish but have everlasting life."

Jesus died on the cross to set people free from sin, and He rose from the grave to provide His gift of eternal life. Romans 6:23 says,

> "For the wages of sin is death, but the gift of God is
> eternal life in Christ Jesus our Lord."

In His grace and love, God has made the way to forgive our sins and to give us eternal life. All we must do to receive healing from the brokenness of sin is to trust in what Jesus has already done for us. In Acts 16:31, God's Word tells us how to be saved from our sin:

> "Believe on the Lord Jesus Christ, and you will be
> saved."

Your greatest problem – the problem of sin and separation from God – is solved when you turn from your sin and ask Jesus to save you. Jesus will give you peace where you once had doubt and fear. His love will replace the feelings of rejection or loneliness you may have felt. Most importantly, He will give you a certainty that you have been forgiven by God and that you will spend eternity with Him in Heaven.

You can trust Jesus for salvation by praying a prayer like this one:

Dear God,

I realize I am a sinner. I know my sin separates me from
You, and I can do nothing to save myself. Right now,
I trust in Your Son, Jesus, who died on the cross for me
to save me from my sin and who rose from the dead to
give me Your gift of eternal life.

Come into my life, Jesus. I invite you to take control of
my life and make me the person You want me to be.
Thank you for loving me and saving me now.

In Jesus' name I pray,

Amen.

If you prayed this prayer and meant it, God promises
in Romans 10:13*:*

> "Whoever calls on the name of the LORD shall be
> saved."

Being saved means that your sins have been forgiven,
that you have a home with God in Heaven when your life
is over, that you have God's Holy Spirit living inside of you
to help you live for Him, and that Jesus will never leave you.

Being saved also means that God's power and presence
are available to you to help overcome the hurts in your life. I

would love to encourage you as you grow in your relation-
ship with Jesus. Please contact our ministry at:

> MOVING FORWARD
> 14613 N. MAY AVE.
> OKLAHOMA CITY, OK 73134
> (855) 436–2961

We want to help you take your next steps with Jesus.

About the Author

Stephen Rummage (M.Div., Southeastern Baptist Theological Seminary; Ph.D., New Orleans Baptist Theological Seminary) is the Senior Pastor of Quail Springs Baptist Church in Oklahoma City, Oklahoma. He is the founder of Moving Forward, a radio teaching ministry which airs daily nationwide. Before moving to Oklahoma, Stephen pastored churches in Florida, North Carolina, Virginia, and Louisiana. He has been a professor of preaching at Southeastern Seminary and New Orleans Seminary, and currently serves on the faculty of Midwestern Baptist Theological Seminary. Stephen and his wife, Michele, have one son, Joshua, who lives in Florida with his wife, Morgan.